GUIDE TO THE PROCESS
BOOKS AND MORE



**Written by and Designed by**
**Cassandra Y. Teague**

GUIDE TO THE PROCESS

BOOKS AND MORE

# Credit Card Guidebook

**A helpful guide to guide you through to a process you can trust.**

TABLE OF CONTENTS:



To be clear, I have no affiliations with any creditors or credit bureaus. I offer more than ten years of experience in the field of credit cards.

## *Welcome*

**Whether you're a seasoned cardholder or new to managing your finances, the strategies outlined in this book will empower you to make informed decisions. You'll find tips on how to maximize rewards, manage your credit score, and leverage the benefits that credit cards offer without falling into common pitfalls.**

**By setting realistic spending limits and tracking your expenses, you will not only safeguard your financial future but also build a solid foundation for achieving your financial goals. This guide is designed to be your companion on the journey to financial literacy and freedom, providing you with the tools needed to navigate the complex world of credit with confidence.**

**Start today by embracing these best practices, and transform the way you interact with your credit cards. Your financial health is within your reach, and with the right knowledge and habits, you can ensure that your credit cards work for you, not against you.**

**To clarify, I am not associated with any creditors or credit bureaus. I have accumulated more than ten years of experience in the credit card industry.**

GT TP
GUIDE TO THE PROCESS
BOOKS AND MORE

# *Key Credit Reporting Agencies*

1. **Equifax**
Website: [equifax.com](http://equifax.com)
Customer Service: 800-916-8800
Equifax is one of the three major credit reporting agencies that provide comprehensive credit reports.

1. **Experian**
Website: [experian.com](http://experian.com)i
Customer Service: 888-397-3742
Experian offers tools and resources to help you understand your credit score and how to improve it.

1. **TransUnion**
Website: [transunion.com](http://transunion.com)
Customer Service: 800-916-8800
TransUnion provides credit reports and scores, along with identity theft protection services.

1. **Innovis**
Website: [innovis.com](http://innovis.com)
Customer Service: 866-712-0021
Although less well-known, Innovis is another credit reporting agency that provides consumer credit information.

1. **ChexSystems**
Website: [chexsystems.com](http://chexsystems.com)
Customer Service: 800-428-9623
ChexSystems specializes in providing banks and credit unions with reports on consumers' banking histories.

1. **Dun & Bradstreet**
Website: [dnb.com](http://dnb.com)
Dun & Bradstreet is known for its business credit reporting, helping businesses establish and grow their creditworthiness.

**Lexis Nexis**
Website: https://consumer.risk.lexisnexis.com/consumer
Customer Service: 1-866-897-8126
Reports: C.L.U.E Report, Real State, Liens, Jugdements and more

Remember, monitoring your credit report regularly can help you maintain a healthy credit score and avoid identity theft. Always ensure your information is correct and dispute any inaccuracies you find.

## Factors that Affect Your Credit Score

Creditwise.com supplied the data for the following charts:
The charts displayed below are derived from information gathered from Creditwise.com, a credit monitoring service, and the TransUnion credit bureau for the year 2023.

### *Impact On Score*

#### *The Importance of Paying on Time*

| | |
|---|---|
| Excellent | 100% |
| Good | 98%-99% |
| Average | 90%-97% |
| Below Average | 90% |

#### *What makes this significant?*

Timely payments are crucial in credit management to maintain a positive credit score. Late payments exceeding 30 days can harm your credit history and report to credit bureaus.

#### *Credit Tip:*

To prevent missing payments, consider setting up autopay or establishing bill pay reminders to receive notifications when your bills are due.

#### *Longest-standing Credit Account*

| | |
|---|---|
| Excellent | 25+ years |
| Good | 8-24 years |
| Average | 3-7 years |
| Below Average | 0-2 years |

#### *What makes this significant?*

The age of your oldest credit card account reflects your credit handling experience and can be used by lenders to evaluate your creditworthiness.

#### *Credit Tip:*

Maintaining your oldest account in good standing can contribute to a healthy credit history.

## Factors that Impact Credit Scores

Creditwise.com supplied the data for the following charts:
The charts displayed below are derived from information gathered from Creditwise.com, a credit monitoring service, and the TransUnion credit bureau for the year 2023.

### Understanding Credit Utilization

| | |
|---|---|
| Excellent | 0-10% |
| Good | 11%-30% |
| Average | 31%-60% |
| Below Average | 61-100% |

### What makes this significant?

The Pitfalls of Maxing Out Your Credit
Utilizing too much of your available credit could lead to trouble when you need it most. This could signal to lenders that you're overextended and struggling to make payments.

### Tips for Improving Your Credit:

Using less than 30% of available credit is a good goal. However, using available credit and paying it off monthly may be better than not using credit at all.

### Recent Inquiries

| | |
|---|---|
| Excellent | 0 |
| Good | 1-2 |
| Average | 3-5 |
| Below Average | 6+ |

### What makes this so significant?

**Credit Inquiries: What They Mean for Your Financial Health.**

While having a few inquiries over the course of a year is not unusual, having too many in a short period may indicate that you are applying for multiple credit lines. This could be a sign that you are financially overextended and may negatively impact your credit score.

### Useful Tip for Managing Credit:

Apply for credit only when you need it. If you're shopping around for credit accounts like a mortgage or an auto loan, try to keep your inquiries within a short period. Applying for multiple new credit lines could be seen as an indicator that someone could be financially overextended.

## Factors that Impact Your Credit Score

Creditwise.com supplied the data for the following charts:
The charts displayed below are derived from information gathered from Creditwise.com, a credit monitoring service, and the TransUnion credit bureau for the year 2023.

*Impact On Score*

### New Accounts within the Last Two Years.

| | |
|---|---|
| Excellent | 0-2 |
| Good | 3-4 |
| Average | 5-6 |
| Below Average | 7+ |

### What is the significance of this?

Opening multiple accounts within a short period may lead lenders to question if you are overextended financially.

### Here's a tip to improve your credit score:

To manage credit responsibly, only apply when necessary, pay bills on time, and use the minimum amount of credit required.

### Overall Credit Limit

| | |
|---|---|
| Excellent | $50k+ |
| Good | $15-50k |
| Average | $2.5k-15k |
| Below Average | 0-2.5k |

### What is the significance of this?

Why Having Low Available Credit Could Affect Your Loan Eligibility
If you don't have enough available credit, a lender may perceive this as a sign that you're financially overextended and may have difficulty paying back the loan.

### Useful Tip for Building Credit:

Tips for Using Credit Wisely
Aim to use less than 30% of your available credit, but don't forget that using some available credit and paying it off each month is better than not using credit at all.

## Establishing and Sustaining Credit History

- ***Secured Credit Card***
- ***Secured Loan***
- ***Installment Loan***
- ***Credit Builder Loans***
- ***Monthly Bills Added To Credit Report***
- ***Build Credit Score***
- ***Build your credit file***
- ***Dont Miss Payments***
- ***Non Profit Lending Circles***
- ***Limit How Often Apply For NewAccounts***
- ***Utilization Rate***
- ***Avoid Bad Habits***
- ***Pay Down Revolving Accounts***
- ***Pay all existing Loans On time and off***
- ***Becoming an Authorized User on a Credit Card***

- ***Set up automatic payments to ensure bills are paid on time***
- ***Monitor your credit report regularly for errors***
- ***Diversify your credit mix with different types of credit accounts***
- ***Keep old credit accounts open to lengthen credit history***
- ***Limit credit inquiries to avoid unnecessary hard pulls***
- ***Use secured credit cards responsibly to build credit***
- ***Consider credit-builder loans to establish a positive payment history***
- ***Join a lending circle for community-based credit building***
- ***Pay off high-interest debts to free up funds for other uses***

***Educate yourself on credit terms and best practices to make informed decisions***

# VALUABLE INFORMATION ABOUT BEING A AUTHORIZE USER

An authorized user is a person added to someone else's credit card account to make purchases or obtain account access. Interestingly, an authorized user's credit history is reported to the credit bureau under the primary account holder's name, which can improve their credit score over time.

**Here are some important points to keep in mind when adding authorized users to your credit card:**

- Authorized users are not financially responsible for accounts.
- Any account history will be reported to credit bureaus.
- While there is currently no age limit for adding authorized users to some credit cards, this may vary between companies.
- Adding an authorized user well before they reach 18 years old can help establish a credit history for them by the time they are 18 years old

### Credit Score Management Tips:

- Steer clear of becoming an authorized user on accounts that often maintain high balances and have a history of late payments.
- Be cautious of accounts with significant balances that only make minimum payments; paying more is always advantageous.
- Aim to be an authorized user on accounts that consistently pay their bills on time and regularly pay off balances or exceed minimum payments.
- Keep your total open credit card balances at or below 30%.
- If your credit report shows a high balance from the previous month that negatively affected your credit score, focus on reducing it.
- Your credit score may decrease if you pay off or lower your balance before the next statement closes; make sure it reflects a reduced balance compared to the last statement.

## Essential Information About Secured Credit Cards

- Secured credit cards necessitate a cash deposit, whereas unsecured credit cards offer a credit line without requiring a deposit. Be sure to ask credit card companies about their deposit policies.

- It's important to understand how these deposits work as they directly impact your credit line and future financial flexibility. The deposit typically serves as your credit limit, so if you deposit $500, your spending limit will likely be the same. As your credit history improves, you may qualify for a transition to an unsecured card, which could unlock increased credit limits and potentially better terms. Always inquire about the conditions under which your deposit is refunded and whether it will be returned as a statement credit or via another method, such as a check. These details can significantly influence your financial planning and credit-building strategy.

- Secured cards can be authorized for varying deposit amounts.
- What is the required deposit amount?
- When and in what manner will you get your deposit refund?
- Will your card transition to an unsecured status after a specific period?
- Will the refund of your deposit be issued as a statement credit?
- Will the deposit refund and any limit increase be applied to your account?
- Will you receive the refund as a check?

**Here are two essential steps to establish a credit history:**

- Always make timely payments and strive to pay off the monthly balance, or even more if you can.
- Once you've built a credit history of six months to a year, most people become eligible for an unsecured credit card.

## Quick Definitions: Remember to Examine Your Credit Card's Terms and Conditions

- **Primary Cardholder**
  The person who is financially responsible for a credit card is known as the primary cardholder. This individual owns the account and is responsible for the credit that was used to open it.

- **Secured Card:**
  This is a type of card that necessitates the use of your own funds as collateral when you open it.

- **Definition of an Authorized User:**
  An authorized user is an individual who has a card and the ability to make charges on the account, but is not the primary account holder.

- **Understanding your Statement Cycle:**
  Your statement cycle is the duration between the start and end dates of your billing period. It's the time frame in which a specific amount of charges is accumulated.

- **Definition of an unsecured card:**
  This type of card does not require a deposit to be made.

- **Start Date of Statement Cycle:**
  The day your new cycle begins.

- **Due Date:**
  The specific date by which payment must be made, either on that date or before.

- **Cut-Off Time:**
  A specific time on the due date that marks the latest possible moment for making payments.

- **Understanding Statement End/Closing Dates and Credit Reporting:**
  It's essential to know the date that your billing cycle ends, also known as the statement end/closing date. Your credit report will reflect whatever balance you have at the end of this cycle date.

**Quick Definitions: Don't Forget to Review Your Credit Card's Terms and Conditions**

- **Past Due Fee:**
  A fee that is charged if payment is not paid by its due date and cut-off payment time.

- **Interest Purchases:**
  If purchases are not paid by their due date, a percentage of the total amount will be charged as a fee.

- **Cash Advance:**
  Access extra cash from a credit card with added fees and cash interest charges.

- **Cash Advance Interest:**
  This is the percentage of money/interest charged when a credit card is used for cash advance purposes .

- **International Fee:**
  A charge applied when you travel outside of your country.

- **Introductory Rates on Credit Cards**
  An introductory rate refers to a special interest rate that is offered when you open a new credit card account. This is typically a limited-time offer, such as 0% interest for 15 months, aimed at enticing new customers to sign up for the card.

- **Credit Limit Fees:**
  A credit limit fee is charged when you exceed your credit limit. It's best to check with your credit card company to understand the terms and fees associated with this.

- **Statement Credit Explained:**
  Essentially, a statement credit is a credit that is applied to your statement.

- **Membership Fee:**
  An annual or monthly fee charged for having a credit card.

## Quick Definitions: Don't Forget to Review Your Credit Card's Terms and Conditions

- **Exploring Payment Options:**
  Various Methods to Make a Payment.

- **Credit Card Payment Options:**
  Varying Amounts to Pay

- **Minimum Payment:**
  The minimum payment is the smallest amount that you are required to pay towards your balance by the due date.

- **Statement Balance:**
  Refers to the total balance made during a given cycle.

- **Current balance:**
  Refers to the total amount of money you currently owe on your credit card.

- **Interest:**
  Is the percentage cost of borrowing money or using a credit card, determined by the lender and borrower's credit history.

- **Grace Period:**
  A grace period refers to a specific period of time that you are given before being charged interest on the charges you've made. This time allows you to pay off your balance without incurring any additional charges.

- **Other Payment:**
  Choose the payment amount you wish to pay.

- **Reset Grace Period:**
  It stops the interest from being charged for a cycle on charges that were made.

GUIDE TO THE PROCESS
BOOKS AND MORE

# Things To Know Notes

Check your credit card terms and conditions

Notes

**Card Rewards: Earn Money or Miles with Every Purchase Get rewarded every time you use your card! Whether you prefer to earn cash or miles, every purchase you make can help you do just that.**

GUIDE TO THE PROCESS

BOOKS AND MORE

Connecting Definitions to Words: Pair each word on the left with the appropriate letter that corresponds to its definition on the right.

Primary Card Holder ________

Secured Card ________

Unsecured Card ________

Statement Cycle ________

Statement Begin Date ________

Statement Close/End Date ________

Due Date ________

Cut Off Time ________

A. Credit Line Requires Deposit

B. Deadline for payment: either on or before the due date.

C. A new billing month has started.

D. Account Owner.

E. The deadline for a bill payment.

F. Deadline for Payment

G. The start of a new billing cycle has begun.

H. Credit line without a deposit.

I. A cardholder on someone else account.

GUIDE TO THE PROCESS

BOOKS AND MORE

Connecting Words to Definitions: Pair each word on the left with the appropriate letter that reflects its definition on the right.

Payment Type ________

Payment Option ________

Minimum Payment ________

Statement Balance ________

Current Balance ________

Other Payment ________

Interest ________

Grace Period ________

Reset Grace Period ________

J. Different payment amounts.

K. The amount to pay to stop interest or keep from paying interest.

L. Paying an amount other than what is listed.

M. A period of time given before you have to pay interest on charges made.

N. Different ways that payments can be made.

O. Money that you give away when you do not pay statement balance.

P. To stop interest on the next cycle.

Q. The balance that is currently on the account.

R. The smallest amount of payment that can be made.

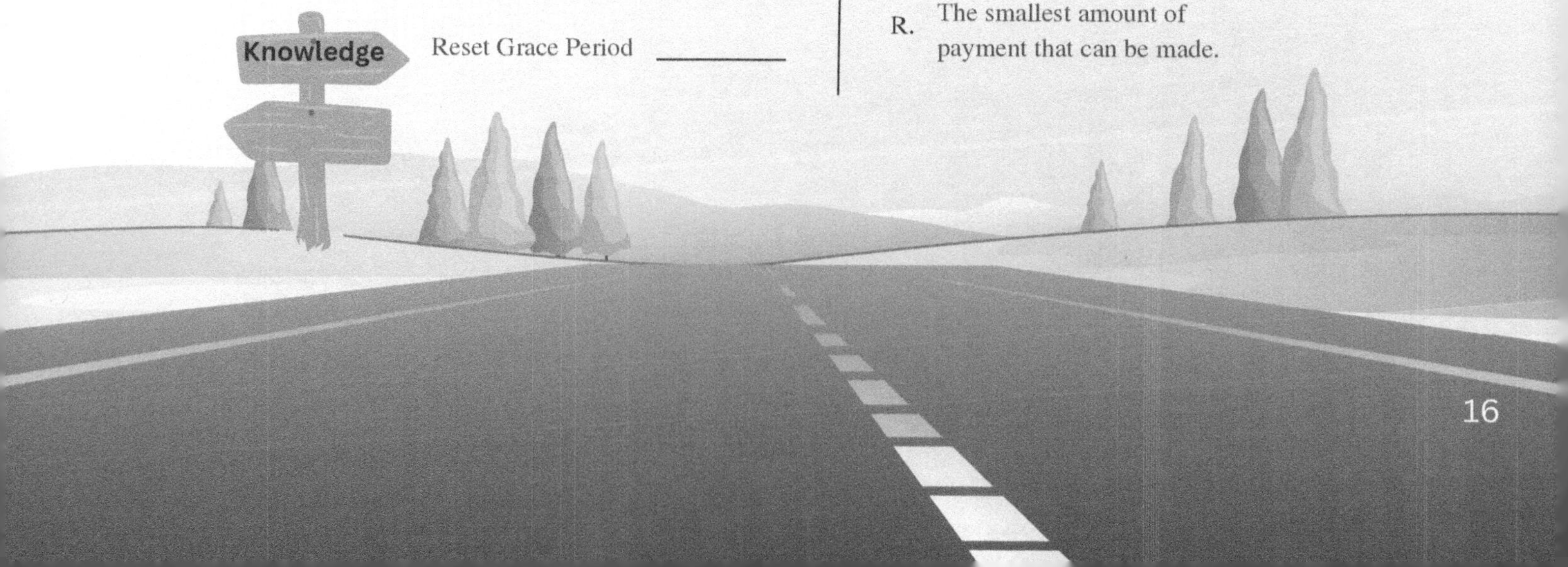

GUIDE TO THE PROCESS
BOOKS AND MORE

Connecting Words to Definitions: Pair each word on the left with the appropriate letter that reflects its definition on the right.

| | |
|---|---|
| Past Due Fee ________ | S. A fee charged for purchases made outside your country. |
| Interest Purchases ________ | T. A interest fee charged for getting cash . |
| Cash Advance ________ | U. Limited of time interest rate |
| Cash Advance Interest ________ | V. A fee charged for not paying charges by their due date. |
| International Fee ________ | W. Fee for having a credit card |
| Introductory Rate ________ | X. Did not payby due date and cut off time. |
| Overlimit Fee ________ | Y. Use a credit card to get cash or a transaction that is considered cash. |
| Statement Credit ________ | Z. Over my credit limit |
| Membership Fee ________ | AA. A credit over the bill |

GUIDE TO THE PROCESS

BOOKS AND MORE

# ANSWER KEY ON NEXT PAGE

## ANSWER KEY Page 15

Connecting Words to Definitions: Pair each word on the left with the appropriate letter that reflects its definition on the right.

| | | |
|---|---|---|
| Primary Card Holder | D | A. Credit line requires a deposit. |
| Authorize User | I | B. The start of a new billing month. |
| Secured Card | A | C. Payment due date: on or before. |
| Unsecured Card | H | D. Account Owner. |
| Statement Cycle | G | E. The date when a bill ends. |
| Statement Begin Date | B | F. The latest time you can make a payment. |
| Statement Close/End Date | E | G. The the beginning and end. |
| Due Date | C | H. Credit line without a deposit. |
| Cut Off Time | F | I. A cardholder on someone else account . |

## ANSWER KEY

### Page 16

Connecting Words to Definitions: Pair each word on the left with the appropriate letter that reflects its definition on the right.

| Word | Answer |
|---|---|
| Payment Type | N. |
| Payment Option | J |
| Minimum Payment | R |
| Statement Balance | K |
| Current Balance | Q |
| Other Payment | L |
| Interest | O |
| Grace Period | M |
| Reset Grace Period | P |

J. Various Types of Payment.

K. Payment Required to Cease Interest

L. Making a Payment that Differs from the Listed Amount.

M. Grace period refers to the length of time during which you can make purchases without incurring interest charges.

N. Various Methods of Payment

O. The Cost of Not Paying Your Statement Balance: Giving Away Your Money.

P. Prevent Interest Charges in the Upcoming Cycle.

Q. The balance that is currently on the account .

R. The smallest payment that can be accepted.

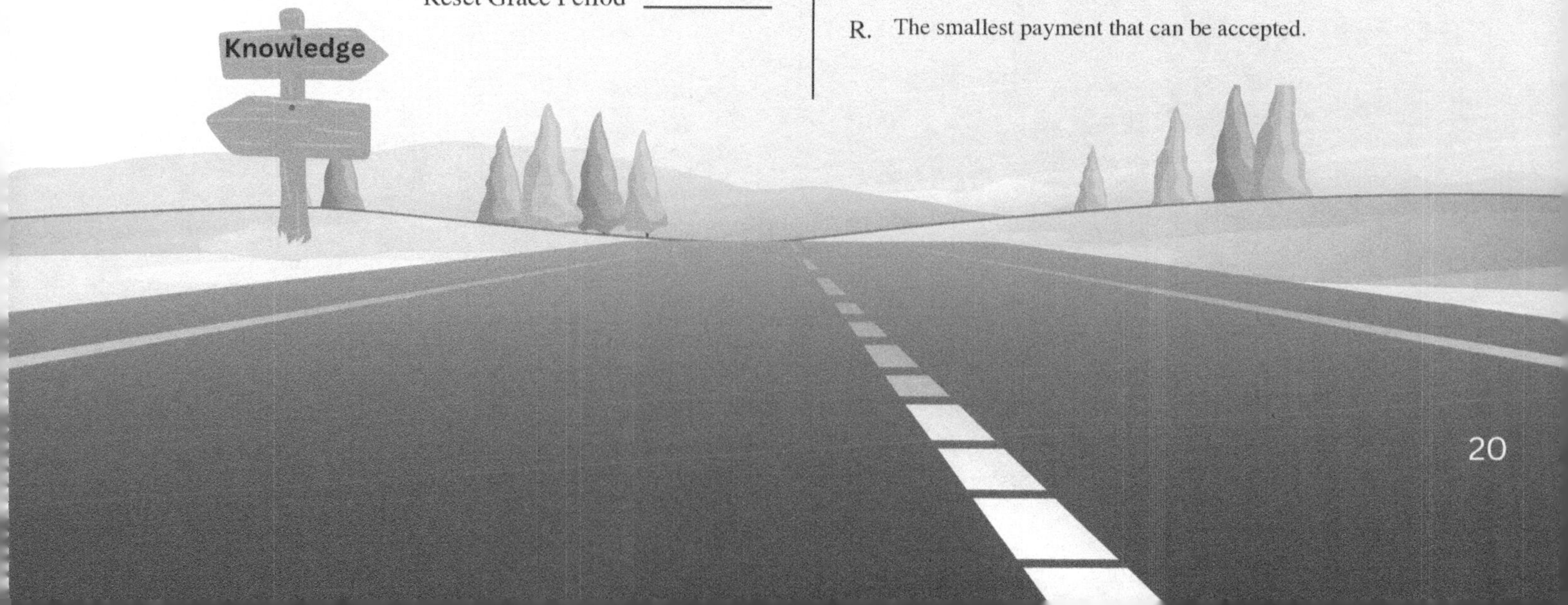

# ANSWER KEY Page 17

Connecting Words to Definitions: Pair each word on the left with the appropriate letter that reflects its definition on the right.

| Word | Answer |
| --- | --- |
| Past Due Fee | X |
| Interest Purchases | V |
| Cash Advance | Y |
| Cash Advance Interest | T |
| International Fee | S |
| introductory Rate | U |
| Overlimit Fee | Z |
| Statement Credit | AA |
| Membership Fee | W |

S. A charge incurred for purchases made outside of your country.

T. A fee is charged for obtaining cash in the form of an interest rate.

U. Limited time offer: Special Interest rates available now.

V. Late Payment Fee Charged for Outstanding Balances

W. There is a fee associated with holding a specific type of credit card.

X. Service Disruption Due to Missed Payment Our records indicate that payment was not received by the due date and as a result, services have been temporarily suspended.

Y. Use a credit card to get cash or a transaction that is considered cash.

Z. For going over my credit limit

AA. A credit on the bill.

GUIDE TO THE PROCESS

BOOKS AND MORE

# INSTRUCTIONS

## Statements

The next pages will teach and show how to better understand statements.

Alot of people never look at their statements. They have know idea when their cycle end or begin. They do not know how much they should pay to avoid interest. The following worksheets will help people have a better understanding.

## Account Statement

Here is a section from a typical credit card bill called the account summary, which provides an overview of your recent transactions, total credits, payments, fees, and credit limits. Using your credit card and paying off the balance in a timely manner demonstrates to the credit card company that you are a responsible borrower. This approach can potentially lead to an increase in your credit limit and help you manage your credit card balance effectively. Conversely, if you barely use your credit card, it may be challenging to obtain a credit limit increase as some credit card companies require evidence of usage before they can approve a limit increase.

Making just the minimum payment on your credit card can also negatively impact your chances of getting a limit increase. Credit card companies may deny an increase if they think the payment is too low. Ideally, you should make charges that you can pay off in full each month. However, if this is not feasible, it's important to make the largest payment you can afford. Making a payment that is too low can affect your ability to get a credit limit increase and put you in debt.

| | | |
|---|---|---|
| 1 | Apr 16, 2022 - May 16, 2022 \| 31 days in Billing Cycle | |
| | **Account Summary** | |
| 2 | Previous Balance | $333.40 |
| 3 | Payments | - $1,128.51 |
| 4 | Other Credits | - $11.96 |
| 5 | Transactions | + $1,046.09 |
| 6 | Cash Advances | + $0.00 |
| 7 | Fees Charged | + $0.00 |
| 8 | Interest Charged | + $0.00 |
| 9 | **New Balance** | **= $239.02** |
| 10 | Credit Limit | $2,200.00 |
| 11 | Available Credit (as of May 16, 2022) | $1,960.98 |
| 12 | Cash Advance Credit Limit | $500.00 |
| 13 | Available Credit for Cash Advances | $500.00 |

Look on next page

## Account Summary Explanation Page 23

1. The billing cycle runs from April 16th to May 16th and represents the period for charging expenses. It's important to note this date for reporting to credit bureaus and planning payment due dates.
2. The previous balance is the amount owed from your last statement and is the balance reported to credit bureaus.
3. Payments made towards the previous balance and additional payments made are also included.
4. Other credits include refunds, fee credits, disputes, and fraud credits.
5. Transactions are the total charges made during the cycle dates listed.
6. Cash advances are all cash withdrawals made during the cycle.
7. Fees charged include late fees and cash advance fees incurred during the cycle.
8. Interest charges on the account summary are applied when charges are not paid in full by the due date or when payments are made past the due date for previous charges.
9. The new balance is the amount owed for the dates listed above the account summary.
10. Your credit limit is the total available credit on your card.
11. Available credit is the credit you had available when your cycle ended.
12. You cash advance limit is the maximum amount of cash you can withdraw.
13. The available cash at the end of the cycle date is also indicated.

## Payment Information

Understanding Your Payment Details on the Bill

The payment information section on your bill provides a summary of all the payments due for the billing cycle that you have recently completed. In this example, the billing cycle is from April 16th to May 16th with a 31-day duration, and the payment is due on June 10th. To avoid interest charges, it is recommended that you pay the statement balance. If you are unable to pay the entire amount, consider making multiple payments before the due date. Alternatively, paying more than the minimum amount may help to reduce the interest you are charged.

**Understanding Credit Card Payments**:

1. The payment due date is the final deadline for paying off the new balance. If you pay the new balance for charges made during this statement cycle, no interest fees will be incurred.
2. Be aware that payments made after 8 pm Eastern Standard Time on the due date will be considered late, so check your statement for specifics.
3. The minimum payment is the smallest amount that can be paid by the due date and cutoff time.
4. The new balance must be paid by the due date to avoid interest, and it is equal to the statement balance.
5. The late payment warning indicates the maximum late fee charge, which can be up to $39.
6. The minimum payment warning reminds you that only making the minimum payment will result in additional interest charges.

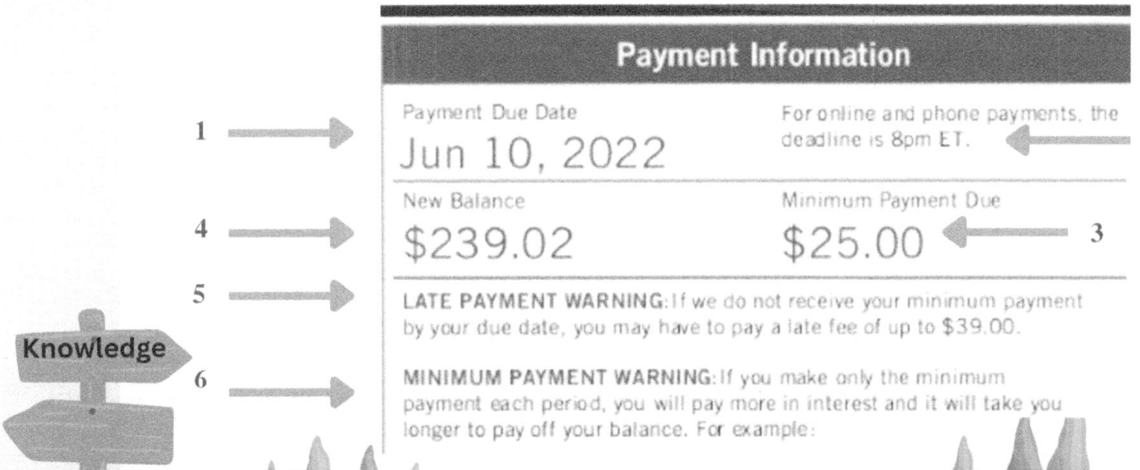

Payment Information

Payment Due Date
Jun 10, 2022

For online and phone payments, the deadline is 8pm ET.

New Balance
$239.02

Minimum Payment Due
$25.00

**LATE PAYMENT WARNING:** If we do not receive your minimum payment by your due date, you may have to pay a late fee of up to $39.00.

**MINIMUM PAYMENT WARNING:** If you make only the minimum payment each period, you will pay more in interest and it will take you longer to pay off your balance. For example:

## Statement WorkSheet

Fill in the blank using the statement.

| Payment Information | |
|---|---|
| Payment Due Date<br>Sep 18, 2022 | For online and phone payments, the deadline is 8pm ET. |
| New Balance<br>$484.60 | Minimum Payment Due<br>$25.00 |

**LATE PAYMENT WARNING:** If we do not receive your minimum payment by your due date, you may have to pay a late fee of up to $40.00.

**MINIMUM PAYMENT WARNING:** If you make only the minimum payment each period, you will pay more in interest and it will take you longer to pay off your balance. For example:

| Account Summary | |
|---|---|
| Previous Balance | $6.98 |
| Payments | - $563.78 |
| Other Credits | - $162.67 |
| Transactions | + $1,204.07 |
| Cash Advances | + $0.00 |
| Fees Charged | + $0.00 |
| Interest Charged | + $0.00 |
| **New Balance** | **= $484.60** |
| Credit Limit | $8,000.00 |
| Available Credit (as of Aug 24, 2022) | $7,515.40 |
| Cash Advance Credit Limit | $1,500.00 |
| Available Credit for Cash Advances | $1,500.00 |

Rewards →

| Earnings as of 08/23/2022 | | | |
|---|---|---|---|
| Previous | $12.44 | Adjusted | $12.54 |
| Earned | $13.04 | Transferred in | $0.00 |
| Redeemed | -$12.54 | Transferred out | $0.00 |
| | | **Rewards** | $25.48 |

1. How much must be paid to prevent incurring interest? ____________

2. What is the minimum payment I can make? ____________

3. What is the due date? ____________

4. What is the cut of time to make payment by on due date? ____________

5. How much rewards were earn this month? ____________

6. How much Fees we're paid? ____________

7. What was the previous balance? ____________

8. How much was charged in transactions /purchases? ____________

9. If $284.00 was paid on October 30th. How much more do I need to pay by September 18th to avoid interest? ____________

10. The transaction/ purchases is 1204.07. Why is the bill only 484.60?

____________________

____________________

____________________

Knowledge

## Statement WorkSheet

Fill in the blank using the statement.

Dec 25, 2022 - Jan 24, 2023 | 31 days in Billing Cycl

**Payment Information**

| | |
|---|---|
| Payment Due Date<br>Feb 18, 2023 | For online and phone payments, the deadline is 8pm ET. |
| New Balance<br>$4,312.32 | Minimum Payment Due<br>$135.00 |

**LATE PAYMENT WARNING:** If we do not receive your minimum payment by your due date, you may have to pay a late fee of up to $40.00.

**MINIMUM PAYMENT WARNING:** If you make only the minimum payment each period, you will pay more in interest and it will take you longer to pay off your balance. For example:

**Account Summary**

| | |
|---|---|
| Previous Balance | $2,490.04 |
| Payments | - $100.00 |
| Other Credits | - $30.60 |
| Transactions | + $1,860.51 |
| Cash Advances | + $0.00 |
| Fees Charged | + $0.00 |
| Interest Charged | + $92.37 |
| **New Balance** | **= $4,312.32** |
| Credit Limit | $8,000.00 |
| Available Credit (as of Jan 24, 2023) | $3,687.68 |
| Cash Advance Credit Limit | $1,500.00 |
| Available Credit for Cash Advances | $1,500.00 |

Rewards

**Rewards Summary** — **Rewards as of: 01/23/2023**

**Rewards Balance** $5.60 — Track and redeem your rewards with our mobile app or on capitalone.com

| Previous Balance | Earned This Period | Redeemed this period |
|---|---|---|
| $27.04 | $26.44 | -$47.88 |

1. What amount needs to be paid to avoid interest? ________________

2. What is the smallest amount I can pay? ________________

3. What date is the due date? ________________

4. What is the cut of time to make payment by on due date? ________________

5. How much rewards were earn this month? ________________

6. How much Fees we're paid? ________________

7. What was the previous balance? ________________

8. How much was charged in transactions /purchases? ________________

9 What was the start date and end for this statement? __________ __________

10. Why was the interest charged on this statement? ________________

11. If $2000 was paid on January 30th. How much more do I need to pay by February 18th to avoid interest?

_______________________________________________

_______________________________________________

GUIDE TO THE PROCESS

BOOKS AND MORE

ANSWER KEY
ON NEXT PAGE

# Notes

## Statement WorkSheet

ANSWER KEY

Fill in the blank using the statement.

**Payment Information**

| | |
|---|---|
| Payment Due Date<br>Sep 18, 2022 | For online and phone payments, the deadline is 8pm ET. |
| New Balance<br>$484.60 | Minimum Payment Due<br>$25.00 |

**LATE PAYMENT WARNING:** If we do not receive your minimum payment by your due date, you may have to pay a late fee of up to $40.00.

**MINIMUM PAYMENT WARNING:** If you make only the minimum payment each period, you will pay more in interest and it will take you longer to pay off your balance. For example:

| Account Summary | |
|---|---|
| Previous Balance | $6.98 |
| Payments | - $563.78 |
| Other Credits | - $162.67 |
| Transactions | + $1,204.07 |
| Cash Advances | + $0.00 |
| Fees Charged | + $0.00 |
| Interest Charged | + $0.00 |
| **New Balance** | **= $484.60** |
| Credit Limit | $8,000.00 |
| Available Credit (as of Aug 24, 2022) | $7,515.40 |
| Cash Advance Credit Limit | $1,500.00 |
| Available Credit for Cash Advances | $1,500.00 |

Rewards

| Earnings as of 08/23/2022 | | | |
|---|---|---|---|
| Previous | $12.44 | Adjusted | $12.54 |
| Earned | $13.04 | Transferred in | $0.00 |
| Redeemed | -$12.54 | Transferred out | $0.00 |
| | | **Rewards** | $25.48 |

1. What amount needs to be paid to avoid interest? $484.60
2. What is the smallest amount I can pay? $25.00
3. What date is the due date? Sept 18
4. What is the cut of time to make payment by on due date? 8pm est
5. How much rewards were earn this month? $13.04
6. How much Fees we're paid? $0
7. What was the previous balance? $6.98
8. How much was charged in transactions /purchases? $1204.07
9. If $284.00 was paid on October 30th. How much more do I need to pay by September 18th to avoid interest? $200.60

10. The transaction/ purchases is 1204.07. Why is the bill only 484.60?

The bill is 484.60 because payments were made before the bill end/close. A payment for 563.78 was made which help lower the bill. There was a creditunder other credit for 162.67. This also lowered the bill balance.

Knowledge

## Statement WorkSheet

ANSWER KEY Page 27

## Fill in the blank using the statement.

Dec 25, 2022 - Jan 24, 2023 I 31 days in Billing Cycl

| Payment Information | |
|---|---|
| Payment Due Date<br>Feb 18, 2023 | For online and phone payments, the deadline is 8pm ET. |
| New Balance<br>$4,312.32 | Minimum Payment Due<br>$135.00 |

**LATE PAYMENT WARNING:** If we do not receive your minimum payment by your due date, you may have to pay a late fee of up to $40.00.

**MINIMUM PAYMENT WARNING:** If you make only the minimum payment each period, you will pay more in interest and it will take you longer to pay off your balance. For example:

TOUCH

| Account Summary | |
|---|---|
| Previous Balance | $2,490.04 |
| Payments | - $100.00 |
| Other Credits | - $30.60 |
| Transactions | + $1,860.51 |
| Cash Advances | + $0.00 |
| Fees Charged | + $0.00 |
| Interest Charged | + $92.37 |
| **New Balance** | **= $4,312.32** |
| Credit Limit | $8,000.00 |
| Available Credit (as of Jan 24, 2023) | $3,687.68 |
| Cash Advance Credit Limit | $1,500.00 |
| Available Credit for Cash Advances | $1,500.00 |

Rewards →

| Rewards Summary | Rewards as of: 01/23/2023 | |
|---|---|---|
| **Rewards Balance**<br>$5.60 | Track and redeem your rewards with our mobile app or on capitalone.com | |
| **Previous Balance** | **Earned This Period** | **Redeemed this period** |
| $27.04 | $26.44 | -$47.88 |

1. What amount needs to be paid to avoid interest? $4312.32
2. What is the smallest amount I can pay? $135.00
3. What date is the due date? Feb. 18th
4. What is the cut of time to make payment by on due date? 8pm est
5. How much rewards were earn this month? $26.00
6. How much Fees we're paid? $92.37
7. What was the previous balance? $2490.04
8. How much was charged in transactions /purchases? $1860.53
9. What was the start date and end for this statement? Dec.25th Jan.24th
10. Why was the interest charged on this statement? The previous balance was not paid in full
11. If $2000 was paid on January 30th. How much more do I need to pay by February 18th to avoid interest? February 18th to avoid interest? $2312.32

Knowledge

GUIDE TO THE PROCESS

BOOKS AND MORE

**Understanding The Payment You Are Making**

ON NEXT PAGE

# Notes

31

## Understanding The Payment You Are Making

When it comes to making payments on your credit card, there are various options available. It's important to understand how each payment type can impact your credit score and credit limit increase. Here are the key things to keep in mind:

- Minimum payments represent the most you can pay on your card. However, only paying the minimum may indicate that you're struggling to manage your balance. If you're paying both the minimum and interest, subtract the interest from the payment to reduce your credit card balance.
- Statement balance payments demonstrate that you can handle the charges on your card and may show credit bureaus that you're paying off your balance. Paying the statement balance will also prevent interest from being charged.
- Current balance payments are similar to statement balance payments, but may include charges that aren't yet due. These charges may be part of a new cycle that hasn't ended yet.
- Other payments are any amounts that aren't the statement balance, minimum, or current balance. Be sure to keep track of when your payments are due to avoid any late fees.

- If I make a payment of $17 on my credit card, taking into account that my interest is $8 and the minimum payment required is $25,

○ **Yes** ○ **No**

Understanding Interest Charges and Minimum Payments on Credit Card Statements
Imagine this situation: Your total bill amounts to $500, and to prevent interest charges, you need to pay the full amount. Instead, you choose to pay just $450.00, planning to carry a balance into the next month. Will this decision result in interest charges and leave you with a $50 balance for the following month?

○ **Yes** ○ **No**

GUIDE TO THE PROCESS

BOOKS AND MORE

## Understanding The Payment You Are Making

Answer On Next Page

Answer Key
Page32

## Understanding The Payment You Are Making

When it comes to making payments on your credit card, there are various options available. It's important to understand how each payment type can impact your credit score and credit limit increase. Here are the key things to keep in mind:

- Minimum payments represent the most you can pay on your card. However, only paying the minimum may indicate that you're struggling to manage your balance. If you're paying both the minimum and interest, subtract the interest from the payment to reduce your credit card balance.
- Statement balance payments demonstrate that you can handle the charges on your card and may show credit bureaus that you're paying off your balance. Paying the statement balance will also prevent interest from being charged.
- Current balance payments are similar to statement balance payments, but may include charges that aren't yet due. These charges may be part of a new cycle that hasn't ended yet.
- Other payments are any amounts that aren't the statement balance, minimum, or current balance. Be sure to keep track of when your payments are due to avoid any late fees.

- If I make a payment of $17 on my credit card, taking into account that my interest is $8 and the minimum payment required is $25,

☑ **Yes** ◯ **No**

Understanding Interest Charges and Minimum Payments on Credit Card Statements
Imagine this situation: Your total bill amounts to $500, and to prevent interest charges, you need to pay the full amount. Instead, you choose to pay just $450.00, planning to carry a balance into the next month. Will this decision result in interest charges and leave you with a $50 balance for the following month?

☑ **Yes** ◯ **No**

GUIDE TO THE PROCESS

BOOKS AND MORE

# A Guide to Due Dates, Billing Cycles, and Splitting Charges

On Next Page

## UNDERSTANDING SPLIT PAYMENT

**A Simple Strategy for Handling Credit Card Debt**

**If you are struggling with credit card debt, this uncomplicated approach may be helpful: limit your charges to a sum that you can pay off within one cycle. Once the new cycle commences, charge the amount that can be paid off and repeat the cycle. Remember to double-check if you are on a floating cycle where the cycle change dates may differ.**

### BILLING CYCLE DATES:
### HERE ARE THE IMPORTANT DATES TO REMEMBER FOR YOUR BILLING CYCLE:

- DUE DATE: THE 15TH OF THE MONTH
- CYCLE END DATE: THE 20TH OF THE MONTH
- NEW CYCLE BEGINS ON: THE 21ST OF THE MONTH

---

**Expert Tips for Managing your Monthly Payments**

**Are you struggling to manage your monthly payments? Here's a helpful guide: If you have a budget of $500.00, it's recommended to charge this amount a few days before the end of your billing cycle, which is typically on the 20th. From the 21st, you can then begin charging again up to your budget for the next billing cycle.**

---

### USING AN EXAMPLE TO ILLUSTRATE: LET'S SAY THAT TODAY'S DATE IS DECEMBER 14TH.

**Effective Management of Credit Card Payments to Avoid Debt**

**To steer clear of accumulating debt, it's essential to monitor your payment cycles and due dates. Your billing cycle runs from November 21st to December 20th, with the first payment due on January 15th. Currently, your account shows a balance of $500.00, and since today is December 14th, it's wise to refrain from making any new purchases until December 21st. This strategy means you won't have to make another payment until February 15th. Focus on settling the $500.00 balance before January 15th to dodge additional interest charges. This plan will not only help you keep a favorable credit score but also prevent debt from becoming unmanageable.**

## UNDERSTANDING SPLIT PAYMENTS

**A Simple Strategy for Credit Card Debt Management**

**Credit card debt can be overwhelming, but there's a simple method to help you manage it effectively. Only charge what you know you can pay off in one cycle, then repeat the process for each new cycle. It's important to check if you're on a floating cycle, where the cycle change dates may vary. With this approach, you can keep your credit card debt under control.**

---

**ESSENTIAL PAYMENT CYCLE DATES TO REMEMBER**

**ENSURE YOU KEEP TRACK OF THESE SIGNIFICANT DATES FOR PAYMENT CYCLES:**

- **PAYMENT DUE DATE: 3RD OF EACH MONTH**
- **CYCLE ENDS: 8TH OF EACH MONTH**
- **NEW CYCLE STARTS: 9TH OF EACH MONTH**

**USING MAY 1ST AS AN EXAMPLE:**

Effectively Managing a $1500.00 Budget for Two Major Purchases

Navigating a $1500.00 budget for two major purchases can be challenging. Follow this strategy to help you stay on track:

- Charge the $1200.00 purchase before the 8th of the month
- Charge the $500.00 purchase after the 9th of the month

By following this approach, you will be able to pay for the $1200.00 purchase on June 3rd and the $500.00 purchase on July 3rd, making it easier to manage your budget.

## A Guide to Due Dates, Billing Cycles, and Splitting Charges

Paying your credit card bill prior to the due date or on time can help you avoid late fees. To prevent late payments, it is important to confirm with your credit card company whether there is a specific cut-off time on the due date for payments. To guarantee timely payment and avoid late fees, it is recommended to make payments before the actual due date. Setting reminders or alerts on your mobile device can assist you in remembering payment due dates, and you can also set up alerts through your credit card companies.

Understanding your billing cycle start date is important for keeping track of when a new cycle begins and when charges are due. Not all charges have the same due date, and it is dependent on the cycle end date. Knowing your cycle end date can help you split your charges and maintain control over your balance. It is important to note that any balance remaining at the end of the cycle will be reported to the credit bureaus.

To split your charges, start by calculating how much you can pay each month for all charges. Then, charge up to just before the cycle end and stop until the new cycle starts. By doing this, new charges will not be at the same time as your previous charges, and it can help when your balance is reported to the credit bureaus.

Determining Lateness in Bill Payment

1. Consider the following scenario: If your payment is due at 5:00 PM EST, and you submit your payment at 5:01 PM EST, would it be considered late?

○ **Yes** ○ **No**

2. If your current cycle is due to end on the 17th, the next cycle will begin on the 18th.

○ **Yes** ○ **No**

3. Clarifying Payment Dates for Credit Card Cycles

Suppose your credit card cycle ends on May 17th, and the payment is due by June 5th. If you made additional charges after May 17th, you might be wondering when those charges are due. Do they need to be paid on June 5th as well?

○ **Yes** ○ **No**

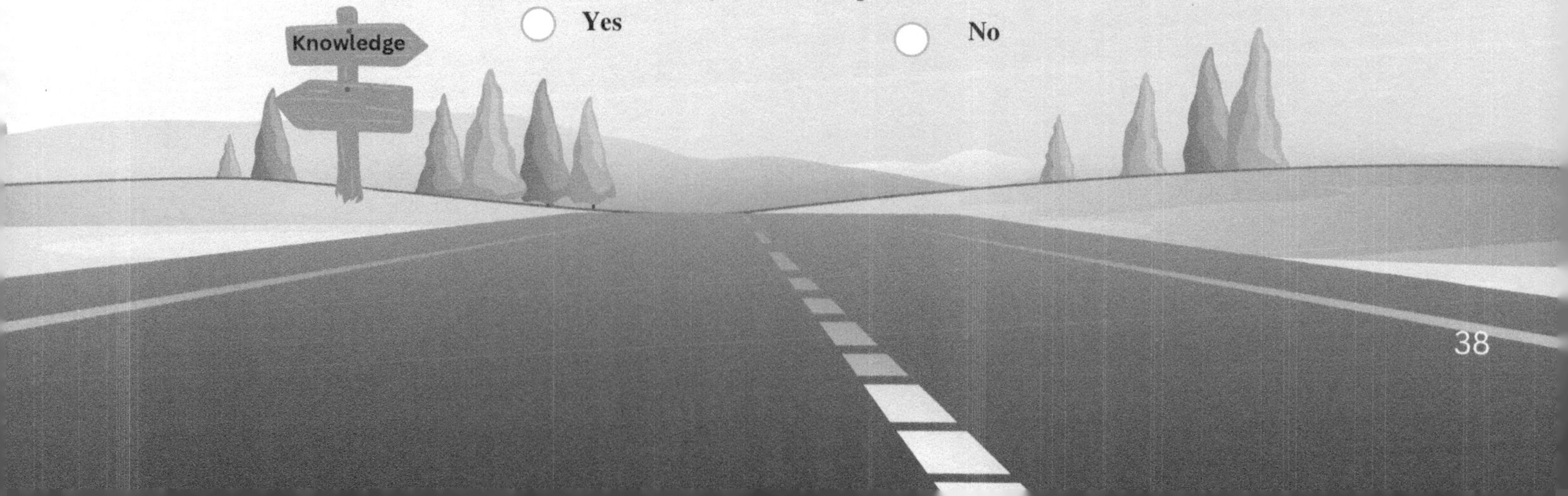

## MULTIPLE CHOICE QUESTIONS

**Answer questions about how you believe you should use your credit card.**

**1) What is a good reason to only pay a minimum payment?**

A. Pay minimum if that is all you can afford.

B. If you want to be in debt.

C. Why pay off your credit card when you can pay the bare minimum.

---

**2) What happens when you pay minimum payment?**

A. You can start to be charged interest and can head down the road towards credit card debt.

B. You are showing credit card companies that you can afford the credit card you were given.

C. You will never be in debt.

---

**3) If your minimum payment is $40 and your interest is $5 and you have a late fee for $20. How much did you pay on the actual credit card balance?**

A. Only $15 went towards your credit card.

B. None of it because the credit card companies wants you to owe them forever.

C. $40 because you do not believe in interest.

---

**4) What can it look like when you pay minimum payment?**

A. It can look like that you can not afford a higher credit limit.

B. It shows you can handle a big credit limit.

C. It can keep you out of debt.

## MULTIPLE CHOICE QUESTIONS

**Answer questions about how you believe you should use your credit card.**

**1) What is the best time to make a payment?**

A. Any day I like because calendars are fake.

B. On the due date or just before due date.

C. You are going out of town, so you can pay your bill when you return.

---

**2) What happens when payments are made on time?**

A. The credit card company throws you a party in your honor.

B. Reports to the credit bureaus as on time payment.

C. You get a standing ovation.

---

**3) What can you do to avoid a late fee?**

A. Call my credit card company and tell them you going out of town and bills are not late when traveling.

B. Call and scream at the agent until they change company policy.

C. Set up an alarm on your phone to notify you a couple of days before the due date. Also setup alerts.

---

**4) How can having a late payment effect you?**

A. It can keep you from getting a credit limit increase.

B. Cause you to be charged interest

C. Both

## MULTIPLE CHOICE QUESTIONS

**Answer questions about how you believe you should use your credit card.**

**1) What is some benefits of paying statement balance?**

A. There is no benefit; the credit card company wants to take my money that they let me borrow.

B. If I spend less than what I earn, my chances of falling into debt will decrease.

C. Paying each statement balance will keep you from paying interest.

---

**2) How can I make it where I can afford to pay each statement balance?**

A. Know your budget and what you actually can afford to pay each month.

B. I use my credit card for things I cannot afford so it do not matter.

C. I do not care about being able to pay balance.

---

**3) Do credit card companies and credit bureaus care about paying the statement balance?**

A. Yes, because it shows credit card companies you can handle what ever you charge on your credit card.

B. No, because the credit bureaus get to see different balance reporting.

C. No, because the grand design is for them to give you credit so that I can use it all to be in debt.

---

**4) Is it better to pay statement or minimum?**

A. Yes, it is better to pay Statement.

B. No, it is better to pay minimum.

GUIDE TO THE PROCESS

BOOKS AND MORE

**A Guide to Due Dates, Billing Cycles, and Splitting Charges**

On Next Page

Answer Key

Answer Key Page 38

## A Guide to Due Dates, Billing Cycles, and Splitting Charges

Paying your credit card bill prior to the due date or on time can help you avoid late fees. To prevent late payments, it is important to confirm with your credit card company whether there is a specific cut-off time on the due date for payments. To guarantee timely payment and avoid late fees, it is recommended to make payments before the actual due date. Setting reminders or alerts on your mobile device can assist you in remembering payment due dates, and you can also set up alerts through your credit card companies.

Understanding your billing cycle start date is important for keeping track of when a new cycle begins and when charges are due. Not all charges have the same due date, and it is dependent on the cycle end date. Knowing your cycle end date can help you split your charges and maintain control over your balance. It is important to note that any balance remaining at the end of the cycle will be reported to the credit bureaus.

To split your charges, start by calculating how much you can pay each month for all charges. Then, charge up to just before the cycle end and stop until the new cycle starts. By doing this, new charges will not be at the same time as your previous charges, and it can help when your balance is reported to the credit bureaus.

Determining Lateness in Bill Payment

1. Consider the following scenario: If your payment is due at 5:00 PM EST, and you submit your payment at 5:01 PM EST, would it be considered late?

- [x] **Yes**
- [ ] **No**

2. If your current cycle is due to end on the 17th, the next cycle will begin on the 18th.

- [x] **Yes**
- [ ] **No**

3. Clarifying Payment Dates for Credit Card Cycles

Suppose your credit card cycle ends on May 17th, and the payment is due by June 5th. If you made additional charges after May 17th, you might be wondering when those charges are due. Do they need to be paid on June 5th as well?

- [ ] **Yes**
- [x] **No**

## ANSWER SHEET AND EXPLANTION

Page 39

**1). What is a good reason to only pay a minimum payment?**

**Answer: A**

It is advisable to pay only the minimum amount required if that is the extent of what you can afford.

---

**2) What happens when you pay minimum payment?**

**Answer: A**

Paying the minimum payment on your credit card can result in accruing interest charges, signaling that you are merely meeting the basic repayment requirement. This practice may ultimately lead to accumulating credit card debt.

---

**3). If your minimum payment is $40 and your interest is $5 and you have a late fee for $20. How much did you pay on the actual credit card balance?**

**Answer: A**

The total payment amount is $15.00. Late fees and interest payments result in a smaller portion being allocated towards the principal.

---

**4) What can it look like when you pay minimum payment?**

**Answer: A**

It appears that establishing a payment arrangement for the outstanding balance is necessary. Your current capacity seems limited to making only the minimum payments, prolonging the process of clearing credit card debts and potentially leading to increased difficulty in managing higher credit limits.

Notes:

## ANSWER SHEET AND EXPLANTION Page 40

**1) What is the best time to make a payment?**

**Answer: B**

It is advisable to remit payments a few days in advance of the due date when making online or phone transactions. Conversely, if sending payments by mail, it is recommended to dispatch them at least 10 days before the due date.

---

**2) What happens when payments are made on time?**

**Answer: B**

Timely payments are communicated to credit bureaus, potentially heightening the likelihood of receiving a credit limit enhancement. Moreover, this practice may lead to offers for reduced interest rates; certain credit cards even incentivize responsible payment behavior with upgrades and additional perks.

---

**3) What can you do to avoid a late fee?**

**Answer: C**

Establishing an alarm on your phone's calendar to prompt payment scheduling can be beneficial. Certain companies provide alert services for this purpose. Additionally, setting up automatic payments is a recommended practice.

---

**4) How can having a late effect you?**

**Answer: C**

Tardiness can have multifaceted repercussions. Punctuality issues can impede your chances of securing a higher credit limit, reflect adversely on your credit report as a late payment, and result in the imposition of interest charges and late fees.

Notes:

## ANSWER KEY AND EXPLANTION Page 41

**1)What is some benefits of paying statement balance?**

**Answer: C**

Paying off the statement balance not only prevents accruing interest but also assists in maintaining a stable financial standing. This practice empowers you to exercise control over your credit card expenditures.

---

**2) How can I make it where I can afford to pay each statement balance?**

**Answer: A**

To effectively manage your finances, it is essential to understand and adhere to a budget. Familiarize yourself with the commencement and conclusion of your billing cycle. Consider dividing your expenses across different billing cycles rather than consolidating them all within one cycle.

---

**3) Do credit card companies and credit bureaus care about paying the statement balance?**

**Answer: A**

Paying your statement balance punctually demonstrates to the credit card company your ability to manage the charges you incur. This practice can potentially facilitate a credit limit enhancement among other benefits. It is important to note that the credit bureaus solely receive information regarding your timely payments and your statement balance at the cycle's conclusion.

---

**4)Is it better to pay statement or minimum?**

**Answer: A**

Unless faced with a financial crisis or benefiting from a 0% interest rate, choosing to pay only the minimum amount on your credit card statement is generally less advantageous than settling the full statement balance. Opting for minimum payments can indicate financial strain, suggesting that you can only manage the essential payment on the outstanding balance. Consequently, demonstrating such limited financial capacity may impede your chances of obtaining a significant credit limit increase.

Notes:

GUIDE TO THE PROCESS

BOOKS AND MORE

# CREDIT BUREAU VS CREDIT CARD

On Next Page

## CREDIT BUREAU VS CREDIT CARD

Learn what effects the Credit Bureaus vs your Credit Card

| QUESTION | ANSWER |
|---|---|
| If you charge/spend over 30% of your limit. Which one is affected by this? | |
| If you only pay a minimum payment but you are under 30% who is affected by this? What are some effects of paying minimum payment? | |
| If you have a $300 credit limit and you spend $100 and pay a minimum payment of $25. Which is affected and how? | |
| If you pay down your big balance before your cycle close. What and why? | |
| What can happen if one month you have a high balance and the the next month you do not? | |

GUIDE TO THE PROCESS

BOOKS AND MORE

## CREDIT BUREAU VS CREDIT CARD

On Next Page
Answer Key

## CREDIT BUREAU VS CREDIT CARD

Learn what effects the Credit Bureaus vs your Credit Card

| QUESTION | ANSWER |
|---|---|
| If you charge/spend over 30% of your limit. Which one is affected by this? | Credit Bureau is affected by this. The reason they want to show you have credit but not exceed 30% of the credit. Another show you have it but you really do not need it. |
| If you only pay a minimum payment but you are under 30% who is affected by this? What are some effects of paying minimum payment? | Credit Cards are affected. Minimum payment means you need to pay the bare minimum on your loan/credit card. It also causes you longer to pay off your credit card. Which means more interest paid out. |
| If you have a $300 credit limit and you spend $100 and pay a minimum payment of $25. Which is affected and how? | Credit Card is affected. Paying $25 on a credit card shows that a payment for arrange needs to be made on paying back $100. This may effect the amount of your credit limit increase. Differentoffers more. |
| If you pay down your big balance before your cycle close. Which is affected? | Credit Bureau and Credit Card. it will report a lower balance to Credit Bureau. This will show to the credit card company you can pay on or off credit card. |
| What can happen if one month you have a high balance and the the next month you do not? | Credit burea: your score might go up for having a to high of a balance. If you bring balance to zero or low as you possibly can itmay bring your score back up. |

GUIDE TO THE PROCESS
BOOKS AND MORE

# The Art of Earning Money through Credit Cards

On Next Page

# Mastering the Skill of Making Money with Credit Cards

Maximizing Your Credit Card Rewards: A Guide

Earning rewards with your credit card is a smart way to make extra cash or accumulate miles for travel. Whether you have a business or personal credit card, you can earn rewards with cash or miles. If you choose cash rewards, you can use them as a credit on your account, receive a check, or sometimes even get a gift card. On the other hand, miles earning cards are best for travel, even though you can also get credit on your account or a check. However, using miles for travel usually gives you a better redemption rate than cashing them out.

To optimize your rewards, avoid paying interest or late fees. Paying extra fees means that your rewards are being used to replace the interest and late fees you are paying. This results in you not getting the full benefit of your rewards and missing out on the full opportunity of making money off your credit card. You can still earn money with your credit card while paying a small amount of interest, but it's best to avoid it altogether to maximize your earnings.

1. If you earned $20 in rewards and your interest charge for the month is $30. Did you make money off your credit card?

   ◯ **Yes** ◯ **No**

2. If you paid your full statement and paid no interest and earned $20 in rewards. Did you make money from using your credit card?

   ◯ **Yes** ◯ **No**

3. If your Apr is 0% introductory rate and your reward bonus is $200.00 if you spend 500.00 dollars. You use your credit card to pay your car insurance which is 600.00 dollars. At this point have you made money by using your credit card?

   ◯ **Yes** ◯ **No**

The questions and answers are the same for Miles rewards.

GUIDE TO THE PROCESS

BOOKS AND MORE

## The Art of Earning Money through Credit Cards

On Next Page

ANSWER KEY

## The Art of Earning Money through Credit Cards

ANSWER KEY Page. 52

Maximizing Your Credit Card Rewards: A Guide

Earning rewards with your credit card is a smart way to make extra cash or accumulate miles for travel. Whether you have a business or personal credit card, you can earn rewards with cash or miles. If you choose cash rewards, you can use them as a credit on your account, receive a check, or sometimes even get a gift card. On the other hand, miles earning cards are best for travel, even though you can also get credit on your account or a check. However, using miles for travel usually gives you a better redemption rate than cashing them out.

To optimize your rewards, avoid paying interest or late fees. Paying extra fees means that your rewards are being used to replace the interest and late fees you are paying. This results in you not getting the full benefit of your rewards and missing out on the full opportunity of making money off your credit card. You can still earn money with your credit card while paying a small amount of interest, but it's best to avoid it altogether to maximize your earnings.

1. If you earned $20 in rewards and your interest charge for the month is $30. Did you make money off your credit card?

   ◯ **Yes** ✓ **No**

2. If you paid your full statement and paid no interest and earned $20 in rewards. Did you make money from using your credit card?

   ✓ **Yes** ◯ **No**

3. If your Apr is 0% introductory rate and your reward bonus is $200.00 if you spend 500.00 dollars. You use your credit card to pay your car insurance which is 600.00 dollars. At this point have you made money by using your credit card?

   ✓ **Yes** ◯ **No**

The questions and answers are the same for Miles rewards.

GUIDE TO THE PROCESS

BOOKS AND MORE

## What Am I Charging

## What Are You Paying Interest On?

On Next Page

GUIDE TO THE PROCESS

BOOKS AND MORE

# INSTRUCTIONS

## What Are You Paying Interest On?

The next page is a questionnaire so that you can see what you are paying interest on.

The objective is to aim for all "no" responses on the list, which includes regular living expenses and personal pleasures such as Netflix, manicures, and others. Some items on the list may already include taxes or fees that you are currently paying, but adding interest to them leads to increased spending.

Indicate "yes" or "no" if you are paying interest, then mark it with a check. Proceed to the notes section to provide an explanation.
Additional questionnaires are available for up to six months.

On Next Page

## What Am I Charging

### Smart Credit Card Usage Tips to Avoid Interest and Late Fees

Using your credit card to pay for monthly bills, such as car in surance and phone bills, can be a great idea. However, if you cannot pay off your statement balance in full, it's best to avoid this practice. Otherwise, you may be charged interest on these bills, adding unnecessary costs. The same goes for fast food or eating out in general. Only charge these expenses if you know you can pay them off in full, as you'll end up paying interest on a cheeseburger. Although putting all purchases on your credit card can help you earn rewards, it's only worth it if you're able to pay your statement balance off. Otherwise, you run the risk of having any rewards you earn wiped out by interest and late fees.Cash advances should be reserved for emergencies only. These advances come with fees and typically do not earn rewards. Be sure to check the credit card terms and conditions to avoid falling into a credit card debt trap.

1. If the only purchases on your credit card are mostly food and your normal monthly bills should you be able to pay your full statement balance?

   ○ **Yes** ○ **No**

2. I took my friends out to eat it cost me 300.00 dollars. I receive my statement. I am going to pay 50.00 dollars this month and pay the whole thing off next month. Am I paying interest on 2 vegan burgers and a steak and a baked potato?

   ○ **Yes** ○ **No**

**What Am I Charging**

If you are unable to settle your credit card statement in full monthly, carefully consider what expenses you would charge to your credit card. Evaluate whether each expense justifies incurring interest charges. Mark with an X the box corresponding to your selection.

| | | |
|---|---|---|
| French Fries | Computer Tablet | Pizza |
| Electric Bill | Shoes | Purse |
| Vacation | Buy A Car | Diamond Ring |
| Phone Bill | Business Equipment | Car Insurance |
| Roof Repair | Pay Taxes | Pool |

GUIDE TO THE PROCESS

BOOKS AND MORE

## What Am I Charging

## What Are You Paying Interest On?

On Next Page

Answer Key

**Smart Credit Card Usage Tips to Avoid Interest and Late Fees**

Using your credit card to pay for monthly bills, such as car insurance and phone bills, can be a great idea. However, if you cannot pay off your statement balance in full, it's best to avoid this practice. Otherwise, you may be charged interest on these bills, adding unnecessary costs. The same goes for fast food or eating out in general. Only charge these expenses if you know you can pay them off in full, as you'll end up paying interest on a cheeseburger. Although putting all purchases on your credit card can help you earn rewards, it's only worth it if you're able to pay your statement balance off. Otherwise, you run the risk of having any rewards you earn wiped out by interest and late fees.

Cash advances should be reserved for emergencies only. These advances come with fees and typically do not earn rewards. Be sure to check the credit card terms and conditions to avoid falling into a credit card debt trap.

1. If the only purchases on your credit card are mostly food and your normal monthly bills should you be able to pay your full statement balance?

   ✓ **Yes** ◯ **No**

2. I took my friends out to eat it cost me 300.00 dollars. I receive my statement. I am going to pay 50.00 dollars this month and pay the whole thing off next month. Am I paying interest on 2 vegan burgers and a steak and a baked potato?

   ✓ **Yes** ◯ **No**

### What Am I Charging

ANSWER KEY Page: 58

If you are unable to settle your credit card statement in full monthly, carefully consider what expenses you would charge to your credit card. Evaluate whether each expense justifies incurring interest charges. Mark with an X the box corresponding to your selection.

| | | |
|---|---|---|
| French Fries | Pizza | ✓ Computer Tablet |
| Electric Bill | Purse | Shoes |
| ✓ Vacation | ✓ Diamond Ring | ✓ Buy A Car |
| Phone Bill | ✓ Car Insurance | ✓ Business Equipment |
| ✓ Roof Repair | ✓ Pool | ✓ Pay Taxes |

GUIDE TO THE PROCESS

BOOKS AND MORE

## What Am I Charging

## What Are You Paying Interest On?

On Next Page

**The goal is for each statement to have more no's.**

Are any of these charges being carried over to a new statement? Mark the ones incurring interest with a checkmark. Consider annotating the reasons for this decision in your notes.

Total=Yes ________

Total=No ________

| What Am I Charging | Yes/No |
|---|---|
| Groceries | |
| Vending Machines | |
| Gastation, or Corner store items. | |
| Any Fast Food or Restaurants | |
| Price Range $1,$5, $10,20 | |
| Hair/ Hair cuts | |
| Any Hygiene Products | |
| Nails/ Pedicure | |
| Any House Cleaning Products | |
| Car payment/ Double Interest | |
| Electric Bill, Water Bill,Gas Bill | |
| Cell Phone Bill/Phone Bill | |
| DMV Renewal/ Driver License | |
| Car Insurance | |
| Car Wash | |
| Netflix/ Amazon/Hulu/ Disney Any Streaming Service | |

The goal is for each statement to have more no's.

Are any of these charges being carried over to a new statement? Mark the ones incurring interest with a checkmark. Consider annotating the reasons for this decision in your notes.

Total=Yes ________

Total=No ________

| **What Am I Charging** | Yes/No |
|---|---|
| Groceries | |
| Vending Machines | |
| Gastation, or Corner store items. | |
| Any Fast Food or Restaurants | |
| Price Range $1,$5, $10,20 | |
| Hair/ Hair cuts | |
| Any Hygiene Products | |
| Nails/ Pedicure | |
| Any House Cleaning Products | |
| Car payment/ Double Interest | |
| Electric Bill, Water Bill,Gas Bill | |
| Cell Phone Bill/Phone Bill | |
| DMV Renewal/ Driver License | |
| Car Insurance | |
| Car Wash | |
| Netflix/ Amazon/Hulu/ Disney Any Streaming Service | |

Knowledge

The goal is for each statement to have more no's.

Are any of these charges being carried over to a new statement? Mark the ones incurring interest with a checkmark. Consider annotating the reasons for this decision in your notes.

Total=Yes ________

Total=No ________

| What Am I Charging | Yes/No |
|---|---|
| Groceries | |
| Vending Machines | |
| Gastation, or Corner store items. | |
| Any Fast Food or Restaurants | |
| Price Range $1,$5, $10,20 | |
| Hair/ Hair cuts | |
| Any Hygiene Products | |
| Nails/ Pedicure | |
| Any House Cleaning Products | |
| Car payment/ Double Interest | |
| Electric Bill, Water Bill,Gas Bill | |
| Cell Phone Bill/Phone Bill | |
| DMV Renewal/ Driver License | |
| Car Insurance | |
| Car Wash | |
| Netflix/ Amazon/Hulu/ Disney Any Streaming Service | |

**The goal is for each statement to have more no's.**

Are any of these charges being carried over to a new statement? Mark the ones incurring interest with a checkmark. Consider annotating the reasons for this decision in your notes.

Total=Yes ________

Total=No ________

| **What Am I Charging** | Yes/No |
|---|---|
| Groceries | |
| Vending Machines | |
| Gastation, or Corner store items. | |
| Any Fast Food or Restaurants | |
| Price Range $1,$5, $10,20 | |
| Hair/ Hair cuts | |
| Any Hygiene Products | |
| Nails/ Pedicure | |
| Any House Cleaning Products | |
| Car payment/ Double Interest | |
| Electric Bill, Water Bill,Gas Bill | |
| Cell Phone Bill/Phone Bill | |
| DMV Renewal/ Driver License | |
| Car Insurance | |
| Car Wash | |
| Netflix/ Amazon/Hulu/ Disney Any Streaming Service | |

**The goal is for each statement to have more no's.**

Are any of these charges being carried over to a new statement? Mark the ones incurring interest with a checkmark. Consider annotating the reasons for this decision in your notes.

Total=Yes ________

Total=No ________

| What Am I Charging | Yes/No |
|---|---|
| Groceries | |
| Vending Machines | |
| Gastation, or Corner store items. | |
| Any Fast Food or Restaurants | |
| Price Range $1,$5, $10,20 | |
| Hair/ Hair cuts | |
| Any Hygiene Products | |
| Nails/ Pedicure | |
| Any House Cleaning Products | |
| Car payment/ Double Interest | |
| Electric Bill, Water Bill,Gas Bill | |
| Cell Phone Bill/Phone Bill | |
| DMV Renewal/ Driver License | |
| Car Insurance | |
| Car Wash | |
| Netflix/ Amazon/Hulu/ Disney Any Streaming Service | |

GUIDE TO THE PROCESS

BOOKS AND MORE

# INSTRUCTIONS

## Payment Help Sheet

The following pages are designed to assist you in staying informed about crucial details concerning your credit cards.

**The objective of the upcoming worksheet is to assist you in monitoring your cycle dates, budgets, and due dates. Specify the amount you can allocate for each month to cover your statement balance.**

**Payment Help Sheet**

**Keep in mind that whatever balance you have at the end of your statement date will be the amount reported to credit bureaus.**

**Statement Month:** July

This is the date to pay charges off by.

Example

**Card Last Four:** 5555 **Due Date:** August 12th

This is the time frame of the charges.

**Begin Date:** June 18th ↔ **End Date:** July 19th

**Monthly Payment Budget: $ 1500**

**To spend for the month that will allow you to pay statement off each month.**

How much can you afford to pay each month? Make sure not to exceed your monthly budget.

**Statement Month:** **Monthly Payment Budget:**

**Card Last Four:** **Due Date:**

**Begin Date:** **End Date:**

Effectively managing your budget for payments can help you settle each statement balance efficiently.

**Payment Help Sheet**

**Keep in mind that whatever balance you have at the end of your statement date will be the amount reported to credit bureaus.**

**Statement Month:** July

This is the date to pay charges off by.

Example

**Card Last Four:** 5555 **Due Date:** August 12th ←

This is the time frame of the charges.

**Begin Date:** June 18th ↔ **End Date:** July 19th

**Monthly Payment Budget: $ 1500**

**To spend for the month that will allow you to pay statement off each month.**

How much can you afford to pay each month? Make sure not to exceed your monthly budget.

**Statement Month:** **Monthly Payment Budget:**

**Card Last Four:** **Due Date:**

**Begin Date:** **End Date:**

Effectively managing your budget for payments can help you settle each statement balance efficiently.

**Payment Help Sheet**

**Keep in mind that whatever balance you have at the end of your statement date will be the amount reported to credit bureaus.**

**Statement Month:** This is the date to pay charges off by.

**Card Last Four:** **Due Date:** ←

This is the time frame of the charges.

**Begin Date:** ↔ **End Date:**

**Monthly Payment Budget:**

**To spend for the month that will allow you to pay statement off each month.**

How much can you afford to pay each month? Make sure not to exceed your monthly budget.

**Statement Month:** **Monthly Payment Budget:**

**Card Last Four:** **Due Date:**

**Begin Date:** **End Date:**

Effectively managing your budget for payments can help you settle each statement balance efficiently.

**Payment Help Sheet**

**Keep in mind that whatever balance you have at the end of your statement date will be the amount reported to credit bureaus.**

**Statement Month:** ______

This is the date to pay charges off by.

**Card Last Four:** ______ **Due Date:** ______

This is the time frame of the charges.

**Begin Date:** ______ **End Date:** ______

**Monthly Payment Budget:**

**To spend for the month that will allow you to pay statement off each month.**

How much can you afford to pay each month? Make sure not to exceed your monthly budget.

**Statement Month:** ______ **Monthly Payment Budget:** ______

**Card Last Four:** ______ **Due Date:** ______

______

**Begin Date:** ______ **End Date:** ______

Effectively managing your budget for payments can help you settle each statement balance efficiently.

## Payment Help Sheet

**Keep in mind that whatever balance you have at the end of your statement date will be the amount reported to credit bureaus.**

**Statement Month:** ____________ This is the date to pay charges off by.

**Card Last Four:** ____________ **Due Date:** ____________ ←

This is the time frame of the charges.

**Begin Date:** ____________ ↔ **End Date:** ____________

**Monthly Payment Budget:**
**To spend for the month that will allow you to pay statement off each month.**

How much can you afford to pay each month? Make sure not to exceed your monthly budget.

**Statement Month:** ____________ **Monthly Payment Budget:** ____________

**Card Last Four:** ____________ **Due Date:** ____________

____________

**Begin Date:** ____________ **End Date:** ____________

Effectively managing your budget for payments can help you settle each statement balance efficiently.

## Payment Help Sheet

**Keep in mind that whatever balance you have at the end of your statement date will be the amount reported to credit bureaus.**

**Statement Month:**

This is the date to pay charges off by.

**Card Last Four:** ______ **Due Date:** ______ ←

This is the time frame of the charges.

**Begin Date:** ______ ↔ **End Date:** ______

**Monthly Payment Budget:**

**To spend for the month that will allow you to pay statement off each month.**

How much can you afford to pay each month? Make sure not to exceed your monthly budget.

**Statement Month:** ______ **Monthly Payment Budget:** ______

**Card Last Four:** ______ **Due Date:** ______

______

**Begin Date:** ______ **End Date:** ______

Effectively managing your budget for payments can help you settle each statement balance efficiently.

## Payment Help Sheet

**Keep in mind that whatever balance you have at the end of your statement date will be the amount reported to credit bureaus.**

**Statement Month:**

This is the date to pay charges off by.

**Card Last Four:** **Due Date:** ←

This is the time frame of the charges.

**Begin Date:** ⟷ **End Date:**

**Monthly Payment Budget:**

**To spend for the month that will allow you to pay statement off each month.**

How much can you afford to pay each month? Make sure not to exceed your monthly budget.

**Statement Month:** **Monthly Payment Budget:**

**Card Last Four:** **Due Date:**

**Begin Date:** **End Date:**

Effectively managing your budget for payments can help you settle each statement balance efficiently.

## Payment Help Sheet

**Keep in mind that whatever balance you have at the end of your statement date will be the amount reported to credit bureaus.**

**Statement Month:**

This is the date to pay charges off by.

**Card Last Four:** **Due Date:**

This is the time frame of the charges.

**Begin Date:** **End Date:**

**Monthly Payment Budget:**

**To spend for the month that will allow you to pay statement off each month.**

How much can you afford to pay each month? Make sure not to exceed your monthly budget.

**Statement Month:** **Monthly Payment Budget:**

**Card Last Four:** **Due Date:**

**Begin Date:** **End Date:**

Effectively managing your budget for payments can help you settle each statement balance efficiently.

## Payment Help Sheet

**Keep in mind that whatever balance you have at the end of your statement date will be the amount reported to credit bureaus.**

**Statement Month:**

This is the date to pay charges off by.

**Card Last Four:** **Due Date:**

This is the time frame of the charges.

**Begin Date:** **End Date:**

**Monthly Payment Budget:**

**To spend for the month that will allow you to pay statement off each month.**

How much can you afford to pay each month? Make sure not to exceed your monthly budget.

**Statement Month:** **Monthly Payment Budget:**

**Card Last Four:** **Due Date:**

**Begin Date:** **End Date:**

Effectively managing your budget for payments can help you settle each statement balance efficiently.

## Payment Help Sheet

**Keep in mind that whatever balance you have at the end of your statement date will be the amount reported to credit bureaus.**

**Statement Month:** This is the date to pay charges off by.

**Card Last Four:** ____ **Due Date:** ____ ←

This is the time frame of the charges.

**Begin Date:** ____ ⟷ **End Date:** ____

**Monthly Payment Budget:**
**To spend for the month that will allow you to pay statement off each month.**

How much can you afford to pay each month? Make sure not to exceed your monthly budget.

**Statement Month:** ____ **Monthly Payment Budget:** ____

**Card Last Four:** ____ **Due Date:** ____

____

**Begin Date:** ____ **End Date:** ____

Effectively managing your budget for payments can help you settle each statement balance efficiently.

## Payment Help Sheet

**Keep in mind that whatever balance you have at the end of your statement date will be the amount reported to credit bureaus.**

**Statement Month:**

This is the date to pay charges off by.

**Card Last Four:** **Due Date:**

This is the time frame of the charges.

**Begin Date:** **End Date:**

**Monthly Payment Budget:**

**To spend for the month that will allow you to pay statement off each month.**

How much can you afford to pay each month? Make sure not to exceed your monthly budget.

**Statement Month:** **Monthly Payment Budget:**

**Card Last Four:** **Due Date:**

**Begin Date:** **End Date:**

Effectively managing your budget for payments can help you settle each statement balance efficiently.

GUIDE TO THE PROCESS

BOOKS AND MORE

# NOTES

GUIDE TO THE PROCESS
BOOKS AND MORE

# NOTES

GUIDE TO THE PROCESS

BOOKS AND MORE

# NOTES

GUIDE TO THE PROCESS
BOOKS AND MORE

# NOTES

GUIDE TO THE PROCESS

BOOKS AND MORE

# NOTES

GUIDE TO THE PROCESS
BOOKS AND MORE

# NOTES

GUIDE TO THE PROCESS
BOOKS AND MORE

# NOTES

GUIDE TO THE PROCESS

BOOKS AND MORE

# NOTES

GUIDE TO THE PROCESS
BOOKS AND MORE

# NOTES

GUIDE TO THE PROCESS
BOOKS AND MORE

# NOTES

GUIDE TO THE PROCESS
BOOKS AND MORE

# NOTES

GUIDE TO THE PROCESS
BOOKS AND MORE

# NOTES

GUIDE TO THE PROCESS
BOOKS AND MORE

# NOTES

GUIDE TO THE PROCESS
BOOKS AND MORE

# NOTES

GUIDE TO THE PROCESS

BOOKS AND MORE

# NOTES

Made in United States
Cleveland, OH
05 November 2026

47675531R00052